Searching the Bible for
Mother God

Examining the Teachings of the
World Mission Society Church of God

Created by

God From the Machine

God From the Machine Blog:

godfromthemachineblog.wordpress.com

www.facebook.com/godfromthemachineblog

Searching the Bible for Mother God

And he gave the apostles, the prophets, the evangelists, the shepherds and teachers, to equip the saints for the work of ministry, for building up the body of Christ, until we all attain to the unity of the faith and of the knowledge of the Son of God, to mature manhood, to the measure of the stature of the fullness of Christ, so that we may no longer be children, tossed to and fro by the waves and carried about by every wind of doctrine, by human cunning, by craftiness in deceitful schemes. Rather, speaking the truth in love, we are to grow up in every way into him who is the head, into Christ

Ephesians 4:11-15

CHAPTER 1

The World Mission Society Church of God – The One True Church?

*** Who is Mother God? Who is Christ Ahnsahnghong? ***

In the past few years, several people have shared with me that they've been approached by members of a church that shared about their belief in "Mother God." Many of the encounters took place on the Rutgers University campus or in other northern New Jersey locations, often being approached in stores like Home Depot or Rite Aid. The people I know who had encounters with these people came to refer to these people as the "Mother God Cult."

Recently, I've learned this "Mother God Cult" is actually the World Mission Society Church of God. If I didn't know better, the name of the church wouldn't have caught my attention much; I probably would've figured it was just another denomination or branch of churches I've never heard of before.

Based on their website, the home church in South Korea appears to be simply called the Church of God. (For simplicity's sake, I'll just use "WMSCOG" from here on out to refer to the World Mission Society Church of God/Church of God throughout this book.)

Within the past few months, I've come into closer contact with the WMSCOG. A housemate of some friends started dating a young woman who is a member of the WMSCOG, and this young man has now stopped attending an evangelical Christian church and has become deeply involved in the WMSCOG. I have since learned that he married the young woman. All this happened in a matter of months.

Shortly after, I found out a student in my high school classroom where I work grew up in the WMSCOG and is currently a member. I learned of this because the student had invited another student of mine to a WMSCOG church service. He accepted, not realizing the WMSCOG wasn't a traditional Christian church. Startled and disturbed by their teachings, he later shared with me his experience. One thing he shared was that he was pressured into being baptized while he was there.

Considering all of this, I decided it was time to look deeper into the WMSCOG. Some people have provided my blog with links to websites criticizing the WMSCOG, mostly by former members, but I decided first, before considering what critics have to say about the WMSCOG, to let the WMSCOG speak for itself.

Before I read any criticisms of the WMSCOG, I visited the WMSCOG's own website to see how they explained their own beliefs. Let it be noted that at the time of the writing of this book, I have not looked at any other websites concerning the WMSCOG. This book is a response strictly to the WMSCOG's beliefs as explained on their own website: http://usa.watv.org/

__A Statement of Concern__

Please note: This isn't an exercise in "I'm right" and "You're wrong." I'm engaging these questions on whether certain churches are teaching a distorted Gospel because

Jesus Christ's true Gospel alone saves us from eternal separation from God. I believe what the writers of the Bible teach, which is that all people are made in God's image and are of eternal worth to God, and neither God nor I wish to see anyone live apart from Him.

Secondly, the purpose of this book is not to argue whether certain churches, sects, or religious groups are "cults" or not. This book is to inform the reader and respond to specific teachings of the WMSCOG. To argue whether the WMSCOG is a "cult" or not is not our concern here, and would only distract from an honest, biblical analysis of the WMSCOG's beliefs.

For the reader's general knowledge, there are two articles in the appendix at the back of this book concerning cults. One explores the difference between a "Christian" cult and a Christian denomination, and the other gives tips on interacting and responding to cult members in general.

You, the reader, may want to pause here to read those articles before moving on or wait until reading the rest of this book. Either way, they are included because I believe the information will benefit you one way or another.

Overview: The Beliefs of the Church of God

As stated earlier, all information concerning the WMSCOG is from their own website (http://usa.watv.org/), and I have made every effort to present it as honestly as possible as I understand it.

The WMSCOG explains history as three 2,000-year eras with 3 saviors, a savior for each era: The Age of God the Father (Jehovah), the Age of God the Son (Jesus), and the

Age of the Holy Spirit (Ahnsahnghong). Ahnsahnghong, a Korean man, was the 2nd Coming of Jesus Christ, though he has since died. Despite this, we're now in the Age of the Holy Spirit.

According to the WMSCOG, without accepting the current savior, Ahnsahnghong, we will not have salvation. Thus, Jesus Christ alone is not enough: "...salvation will never be given to those who are stuck on the name of Jesus in this age." We must accept "Christ Ahnsahnghong" for salvation in this age and pray in his name.

The WMSCOG partakes in seven "feasts" or ritual celebrations throughout the year. All seven of these have grounds in the Old Testament, but, according to the WMSCOG, each of them should've been practiced throughout all three ages in slightly different forms. For example, the WMSCOG has a yearly mass gathering where they partake in the "Passover," though it appears to more closely resemble the Lord's Supper. Other examples include the Day of First Fruits/Resurrection Day and the Feast of Weeks/Pentecost. Partaking in the WMSCOG's version of the Passover is required for salvation.

The WMSCOG also believes in Mother God, who is also called Jerusalem Mother. She is "the Second Coming Jesus' [Ahnsahnghong's] wife." Jesus didn't give his people eternal life 2,000 years ago because he was waiting for the appearance of his wife, through whom eternal life will come. God the Mother is currently living in South Korea.

In a video on the website, Mother God is shown at the New Jerusalem Temple in Korea, surrounded by many happy, well-dressed admirers. The video shows her holding their hands, walking with them, and hugging them. In a testimony, Nathan from Memphis, USA, says, "This is the place where our heavenly mother dwells, the land of prophecy, so I came here to receive the water of life that you can only receive here in Korea from God the Mother." A female Korean teen states, "If God the Mother does not exist, there would be no happiness in the world."

The WMSCOG website clearly teaches that eternal life can only come through Mother God.

History: The Church of God

The WMSCOG was started in South Korea. Here is a brief overview of their history as given on their website:

1948 – Baptism of Christ Ahnsahnghong "according to the prophecy of King David."

1964 – Christ Ahnsahnghong established the Church of God.

Feb. 1985 – Christ Ahnsahnghong "ascended" (which we can assume means he died).

1987 – Twenty WMSCOG churches established in Korea.

Late 90's- early 2000's – Church spreads outside of Korea to several countries, including to the USA in LA.

Sept. 2000 – Completed New Jerusalem Temple in Bundang-gu, Seongnam, South Korea.

Dec. 2000 – New York church established.

2008 – One million members registered worldwide.

2009 – 2nd NY church established.

*Oddly, nothing in their history on their website mentions Mother God.

CHAPTER 2

5 Tips for Understanding the Bible

Throughout the WMSCOG's explanation of their beliefs on their website, they cite a multitude of verses from the Bible as justification for these beliefs. The WMSCOG's use of Scripture clearly shows they believe, like the author of this book, in the divine authority of Scripture and that the Bible is the Word of God.

Since this book will be looking closely at the Bible verses used by the WMSCOG, it's a good idea to spend a chapter discussing how to do biblical interpretation. Much of this book will be analyzing Scripture, so having a good base at the start is essential. Below are six tips for understanding God's Word.

#1 - Allow the Bible to speak for itself!

We all have baggage, biases, and assumptions we bring with us everywhere we go and are involved in everything we do, whether we realize it or not. Still, we should work towards allowing the Bible to speak for itself, and we should be careful not to impose our views on the text rather than letting the text speak for itself (no matter how well we think we know it)!

Honest biblical interpretation reads the text as it is and works to understand what the author was communicating to his original audience. Interpretation is not: "This is what

I think. Now let me look through the Bible and find verses to support my view."

#2 - Context! Context! Context!

We've all had situations where someone quotes a Bible verse to prove a point, and it sounds pretty darn convincing – though something also doesn't sound quite right. Then, later, when we read the whole section the quoted verse appears in, we discover the section had nothing to do with what the person was talking about! The person took the verse totally out of context! One of the biggest errors of Christians (and even non-Christians trying to use the Bible to argue against Christians) is to grab random Bible verses out of context to "prove" the opinions they're promoting.

In fact, in some circles, this is the norm; any opinion can be "proved" by citing a single verse. Remember this essential rule of proper interpretation: *context, context, context!*

If anyone (whether it's a friend, a trusted pastor, or the Pope) quotes a Bible verse, and if what they're proposing the verse means doesn't sound quite right, all you need to do is open your Bible and read the verse in context. This means reading the whole section, chapter, or even book in which the verse appears.

For example, if someone claims because of Psalm 148:10 that cattle should be welcomed to worship in churches with humans, you probably should open up to Psalm 148 and read the complete Psalm (and hopefully you have a common sense understanding of the difference between poetic and literal language too). If someone claims Christians should not eat figs because Jesus hates figs, as evident by his curse upon a fig tree in Mark 11 and

Matthew 21, maybe you should take a moment to read the episode and figure out what Jesus was truly teaching in carrying out this action.

Yes, both examples above are absurd, but they illustrate how verses or passages can be made to mean silly things they don't actually say. Context, context, context!

(*Since I will be citing a lot of Scripture throughout this book, I encourage you to take time to read everything I cite in context so you can judge for yourself whether I am correctly representing the Bible or not.)

#3 - Scripture interprets Scripture!

The Bible is by no means a simple read. We all come across passages that perplex us, and we must wrestle with them. Sometimes we come across passages that seem to teach something very different than what we thought the writers of the Bible taught. For instance, did Jesus really say in Luke 14:26 that in order to follow him a person must "hate" his own family? Yes, he did. But we can't understand Luke 14:26 in isolation away from the other things Jesus taught. Considering Jesus' other teachings, what point was Jesus making?

Remember this rule of thumb: *Clear passages clarify unclear passages.* When puzzled by a verse, find passages that cover similar teachings and read them as well.

Unfortunately, the Bible is not organized in easy-to-find subject-by-subject order. So, Jesus speaks about, say, divorce in Matthew 5, but then he also speaks about it in Matthew 19, and Paul speaks about divorce as well in 1 Corinthians 7. This is why it's important to have a good understanding of the overall story of the Bible. Along with other reasons, it gives you a framework for understanding troublesome sections.

#4 – The Bible is a work of literature!

The Bible is God's inspired Word, yet God used men to write the books of the Bible in various styles and genres over many generations. The Bible contains histories, poetry, prophecy, letters, and more. Understanding what type of genre a specific book or section of the Bible is helps you to interpret it correctly. For example, we can't interpret a parable told by Jesus as a literal, historical event, because parables are fictitious, symbolic tales to illustrate a message.

The Bible being a literary work also means both figurative (poetic) and literal language are used in it. For example, psalms by nature are poetic. Thus, when we read them, we have to be aware that non-literal, poetic language is regularly used. Moreover, in the Gospel of John, Jesus calls himself a light, a vine, and a door. Should we take him literally? Like any work of literature, the reader needs to strive to understand what the author was communicating to his original audience. We understand what to take as literal or figurative language through (once again) context, context, context!

#5 – Have a good translation & study Bible!

Modern English translations are usually split into two groups: literal translations and dynamic translations.

Literal translations attempt to translate the Bible as accurately as possible on a word-by-word basis from the original ancient Hebrew and Greek. The problem is there isn't always an English equivalent for every word or phrase and some literal translations make for some clumpy, awkward reading. The NASB is a literal translation printed today.

Dynamic translations translate idea-by-idea, meaning they're not so much concerned about getting the exact wording, but communicating the essence of the original idea. The good thing is dynamic translations tend to be more smooth and readable, especially if you want to read a large section of the Bible. But because dynamic translations aren't as concerned with the exact wording, much more interpretation is involved in the translating. A dynamic translation may give you only one understanding of a difficult passage, so you may also want to look at a literal translation when wrestling with perplexing passages. The NLT is a popular dynamic translation.

The NIV falls in the middle between literal and dynamic translations, and because of this, it's one of the most popular translations printed today. Personally, I use the ESV as my regular Bible, which is a good literal translation but it also reads well for the most part.

Also, a good study Bible with background information and footnotes is priceless for gaining insight. The ESV and NIV study Bibles are very good.

Finally, two books I recommend for learning about biblical interpretation are *A Basic Guide to Interpreting the Bible* by Robert H. Stein and *40 Questions about Interpreting the Bible* by Robert L. Plummer. Both books are readable and accessible.

A Bit More About (Poor) Biblical Interpretation

Where there are certainly wise ways of interpreting Scripture, there are also unwise ways. Sadly, sometimes poor biblical interpretation is not just unwise but purposely deceitful, where the words of Scripture are manipulated to say what someone other than God wants them to say. We want to avoid these practices at all costs.

Considering what we covered above, below are three poor (or even dishonest) strategies for biblical interpretation:

(1) Imposing views on the text rather than letting the text speak for itself.

We covered this already above in the section about reading Bible verses in context. We can make the Bible say almost anything we want if we isolate verses and take them out of context.

(2) Inconsistent decisions on what should be taken literally or figuratively, often based on preconceived ideas.

Unusual churches with unorthodox teachings have the habit of taking verses usually taken as literal figuratively and verses usually taken as figurative literally. The decisions are often quite random and based on preconceived beliefs.

(3) Selective "translation" and adherence to grammar rules.

Similar to the other erroneous or dishonest strategies above, some unorthodox churches have their own "translation" of the Bible, where they change words and grammar to fit their beliefs. Because of this, be sure to refer to a legitimate Bible translation (such as the ESV or NASB).

A Few Words on the Book of Revelation

The closing book of the New Testament, the Book of Revelation is notoriously difficult to interpret. Even legitimate conservative New Testament scholars break up into three or four major camps on how to understand it. The main reason for this is that Revelation is apocalyptic literature, a style of ancient literature that is highly symbolic.

Unorthodox churches with odd teachings almost universally seize on the ambiguity of Revelation to "prove" their views, interpreting symbols as they see fit. (Further, many of these churches have an unhealthy fascination with the End Times.)

Despite these difficulties, context is (as always) the key. There are things that can be known for certain in Revelation and certain interpretations that definitely can be eliminated. If nothing else, be wary of anyone going to Revelation to "prove" an unusual viewpoint.

(To learn more about legitimate interpretations of the book of Revelation, read *Four Views of the Book of Revelation* published by Zondervan, and/or see Wayne Grudem's *Systematic Theology*.)

And So...

In Ephesians 4:14, Paul speaks of those "tossed to and fro by the waves and carried about by every wind of doctrine, by human cunning, by craftiness in deceitful schemes." We must strive for a correct understanding of the Bible so we are not people upon the waves.

CHAPTER 3

Ahnsahnghong & the 2nd Coming of Christ

Who is Ahnsahnghong? God? Christ? Holy Spirit? All of them?

The WMSCOG makes a lot of claims about their founder, Ahnsahnghong. From the WMSCOG website:

- "For our salvation, God divided six thousand years into three ages: the age of the Father, the age of the Son, and the age of the Holy Spirit, and He allowed a different Savior's name for each of these ages — the name of Jehovah in the age of the Father, the name Jesus in the age of the Son, and the name Ahnsahnghong in the age of the Holy Spirit."

- "Now we are living during the last age of the Holy Spirit. Thus, God has been administrating His plan of salvation, using the new Savior's name, the name of the Holy Spirit--Ahnsahnghong. Salvation is only given to those who believe in the name of the Savior that God has allowed to the people living in that particular age. Because we are now living in the age of the Holy Spirit, we must receive the Holy Spirit, Ahnsahnghong, as the Savior of this age."

- "The name is Ahnsahnghong, Jesus' new name."

- "The God in heaven is our God the Father. Just as we have a physical father on this earth, we have a

18

spiritual Father in heaven. He is God the Father, Ahnsahnghong."

So, it appears from what the WMSCOG teaches, Ahnsahnghong is all of the following: God the Father (Jehovah) and the Holy Spirit; plus, he's God the Son, Jesus Christ, and, thus, also the 2nd Coming of Jesus Christ.

In the next two chapters, we will be analyzing Ahnsahnghong's identity.

Jesus' 2nd Coming: It's No Secret

Is Ahnsahnghong the Second Coming of Jesus Christ?

Since the WMSCOG uses the Bible extensively to explain their beliefs, I will use the Bible to critique their beliefs.

Could Ahnsahnghong possibly be the Second Coming of Jesus Christ? First, let's look at what's written in the Bible about Jesus' Second Coming. The Bible writers clearly teach three facts about Jesus' Second Coming:

(1) Jesus will return in the same way as he left.

(2) Jesus' return will be visual and known by everyone.

(3) With Jesus' return will come the Resurrection of the dead.

Let's look at these three facts closer:

After Jesus' crucifixion, death, and resurrection, he taught his disciples for 40 days and then ascended into heaven. Christians call this event "The Ascension."

Acts 1:9-11:

"And after He [Jesus] had said these things, He was lifted up while they [the disciples] were looking on, and a cloud received Him out of their sight. And as they were gazing intently into the sky while He was going, behold, two men in white clothing stood beside them. They also said, 'Men of Galilee, why do you stand looking into the sky? This Jesus, who has been taken up from you into heaven, will come in just the same way as you have watched Him go into heaven.'"

Before going, Jesus had promised he would return for his believers:

John 14:1-3:

"Do not let your heart be troubled; believe in God, believe also in Me. In My Father's house are many dwelling places; if it were not so, I would have told you; for I go to prepare a place for you. If I go and prepare a place for you, I will come again and receive you to Myself, that where I am, there you may be also."

In the meantime, Jesus' disciples were to spread Jesus' good news of salvation, bringing more and more people to salvation through Christ until he returns. (See the Great Commission in Matthew 28:16-20.)

As the angels say in Acts 1:11, in the same way Jesus left, he will return. It will be visual and known by all:

Luke 21:27:

"Then they will see the Son of Man [Jesus] coming in a cloud with power and great glory."

Revelation 1:7:

"Behold, He [Jesus] is coming with the clouds, and every eye will see Him, even those who pierced Him; and all the tribes of the earth will mourn over Him. So it is to be. Amen."

The bodily Resurrection of the dead is a regular teaching throughout both the Old and New Testament. (Take a moment to read all of 1 Corinthians 15.) In fact, in Matthew 22:23-33, Jesus criticizes the Sadducees, who don't believe in the resurrection. He says they don't understand Scripture or the power of God:

" The same day Sadducees came to him, who say that there is no resurrection, and they asked him a question, ...

"But Jesus answered them, 'You are wrong, because you know neither the Scriptures nor the

power of God. For in the resurrection they neither marry nor are given in marriage, but are like angels in heaven. And as for the resurrection of the dead, have you not read what was said to you by God: "I am the God of Abraham, and the God of Isaac, and the God of Jacob"? He is not God of the dead, but of the living."' (Matthew 22:23, 29-32)

Furthermore, the Resurrection will occur at the Second Coming:

1 Thessalonians 4:16-17:

"For the Lord Himself will descend from heaven with a shout, with the voice of the archangel and with the trumpet of God, and the dead in Christ will rise first. Then we who are alive and remain will be caught up together with them in the clouds to meet the Lord in the air, and so we shall always be with the Lord."

With Jesus' Second Coming and the Resurrection of the dead will also come the Final Judgment. (See Chapters 19-21 of Revelation.) Depending on a person's interpretation of "The Millennium" in Revelation 20:1-6 (which is only taught here in the entire Bible, and even traditional, conservative Christian scholars understand it in different ways), the Final Judgment may occur at the same time as the Resurrection of the dead or later after Jesus' Millennium reign.

Many lean towards the teaching that Final Judgment will happen immediately at the 2nd Coming and Resurrection of the dead, but this does not concern us here or impact our understanding of the 2nd Coming concerning Ahnsahnghong.

Interestingly, Jesus also gives a warning when speaking of his Second Coming. He warns us not to be fooled by frauds claiming to be the Second Coming of Christ:

Matthew 24:23-27:

[Jesus said,] "Then if anyone says to you, 'Behold, here is the Christ,' or 'There He is,' do not believe him. For false Christs and false prophets will arise and will show great signs and wonders, so as to mislead, if possible, even the elect. Behold, I have told you in advance. So if they say to you, 'Behold, He is in the wilderness,' do not go out, or, 'Behold, He is in the inner rooms,' do not believe them. For just as the lightning comes from the east and flashes even to the west, so will the coming of the Son of Man be."

This is particularly interesting because Jesus is confirming, yes, there will be false Christs, even ones that seem real with "great signs and wonders" but don't believe them *because it'll be clear to all when the real Christ comes because of the specific manner of his return.* No one will need to tell us Christ has returned; we will know.

So, let's recap: Jesus will return by descending from the sky to earth; everyone will clearly understand that this is Jesus; and once he returns, the dead are resurrected.

And So...?

Does Ahnsahnghong fulfill any of these biblical requirements of Christ's Second Coming? In fact, does he fulfill even *one* of these biblical truths? How many times have false Christs appeared in history, claiming to be Jesus' Second Coming – only to die later?

There's a very good reason why Christianity has flourished for 2,000 years: Because Jesus died but didn't stay dead.

Moreover, when Jesus returns, he's here to stay.

"Christ" Ahnsahnghong is dead. He's been dead since February of 1985. He's not coming back. He is not the Christ.

CHAPTER 4

Ahnsahnghong & the Trinity

Is Ahnsahnghong the Trinitarian God? Does the WMSCOG have a correct understanding of the Trinity? Do they promote a schizophrenic God?

The World Mission Society Church of God teaches that their founder, Ahnsahnghong, is God the Father, God the Son, and God the Holy Spirit – God in three forms. Before we look at the WMSCOG's teachings, let's look at the traditional Christian understanding of the Trinity.

A Biblical Understanding of the Trinity

Traditional Christianity believes in the Trinity: one God, three persons – God the Father, God the Son, and God the Holy Spirit. This belief is unique to Christianity, and it's certainly a difficult doctrine to wrap our finite heads around, (and, thus, it's a favorite target of those critical of Christianity, often mistakenly accusing Christians of polytheism). Yet, the doctrine of the Trinity is seen throughout Scripture. Furthermore, it is something that we can only know through Scripture, meaning we could only know about God's Trinitarian nature because God has revealed it to us.

In order to understand the Trinity correctly, we need to understand that the three persons are distinct persons yet of the same nature – they share the same divine substance. This means they are one God, and there is *only* one God.

James White's definition of the Trinity in his book *The Forgotten Trinity* is clear and concise:

"Within the one Being that is God, there exists eternally three coequal and coeternal persons, namely, the Father, the Son, and the Holy Spirit."

White goes on to quote Hank Hanegraaff of the Christian Research Institute: "when speaking of the Trinity, we need to realize that we are talking about one *what* and three *who's*."

I find thinking about it like a 1st Century Jew helps. Jews in Jesus' day, unlike the pagan Romans, understood that there was only one God, and everything else is *not* God. Thus, there is God, and there is everything he created, and there is no third category. Thus, when Jesus says he's the Son of God, the Jews don't understand it as Romans and think, "Ok, this guy thinks he's *part* God" or "This guy thinks he's a demi-god," they understand it correctly as Jesus saying, "I am God." That's why they accuse him of blasphemy, a crime worthy of death. To a Jew, something can't be *part* God. Something is either fully God or fully something else.

The Trinitarian nature of God has several implications. In the book *Total Truth*, Nancy Pearcey writes of one of them:

> "The human race was created in the image of God, who is three Persons so intimately related as to constitute one Godhead... both oneness and threeness are equally real, equally ultimate, equally basic and integral to God's nature...

"The balance of unity and diversity in the
Trinity gives a model for human social life,
because it implies that both individuality and
relationship exist within the Godhead itself.
God is being-in-communion. Humans are
made in the image of a God who is a tri-
unity—whose very nature consists in
reciprocal love and communication among
the Persons of the Trinity… the Trinity
implies the dignity and uniqueness of
individual persons. Over against radical
individualism, the Trinity implies that
relationships are not created by sheer choice
but are built into the very essence of human
nature. We are not atomistic individuals but
are created for relationships."

Understanding that God has always existed as three
persons gives new meaning to the biblical truth that "God is
love" (1 John 4:8).

To understand the Trinity, it's best to state the doctrine (as
Wayne Grudem does in his *Systematic Theology*) in three
sentences:

    (1) **God is three persons – Father, Son, and
         Holy Spirit.**
    (2) **Each person is fully God.**
    (3) **There is only one God.**

Denying or changing any of these three statements would
not accurately illustrate the biblical belief of the Trinity. All
three statements must be accepted as truth for correct
understanding of the Trinity.

Moreover, trying to explain the Trinity in any other manner tends to lead to misrepresentations of the Trinity and basically (to use an out-of-fashion word) heresy. Likewise, any analogy to explain the Trinity often proves misleading or inaccurate. As James White states in his book, "If something is truly unique, it cannot be compared to anything else, at least not without introducing some element of error."

An Old Heresy

Now, let's look at how the WMSCOG explains the Trinity on their own website:

> "The concept of 'Trinity' means that God the Father, God the Son, and God the Holy Spirit are not different entities, but are one God. The Trinity—God the Father [Jehovah], God the Son [Jesus], and God the Holy Spirit [Ahnsahnghong]—are one…

> "To better understand the Trinity, let's first consider the transformation of water. Water is a liquid, but when its temperature falls below 0° C, the water will turn into ice, a solid. When the water is boiled, it turns into vapor, a gas. Water, ice, and vapor have different names and different forms, but their substance is the same: H_2O.

> "It is similar to when an actor in a monodrama plays three different characters — a father, a son, and a grandson — all having different voices. Although there are

28

three different voices and three different roles, there is only one actor."

What the WMSCOG is stating here and elsewhere on their website teaches that Ahnsahnghong is God appearing throughout history in three different forms. The WMSCOG breaks down history into three 2,000-year eras where God appears as a savior differently in each one:

(1) The Age of God the Father (Jehovah)
(2) The Age of God the Son (Jesus)
(3) The Age of the Holy Spirit
(Ahnsahnghong).

What the WMSCOG is actually teaching is an old heresy called *Modalism*. The website carm.org summarizes Modalism succinctly:

> "Modalism is probably the most common theological error concerning the nature of God. It is a denial of the Trinity. Modalism states that God is a single person who, throughout biblical history, has revealed Himself in three modes or forms. Thus, God is a single person who first manifested himself in the mode of the Father in Old Testament times. At the incarnation, the mode was the Son; and after Jesus' ascension, the mode is the Holy Spirit. These modes are consecutive and never simultaneous. In other words, this view states that the Father, the Son, and the Holy Spirit never all exist at the same time—only one after another. Modalism denies the

distinctiveness of the three persons in the Trinity even though it retains the divinity of Christ."

According to the WMSCOG, Ahnsahnghong is God the Father, God the Son, and God the Holy Spirit. All of these titles belong to him, and throughout the website he's called "Christ Ahnsahnghong" and even "God Ahnsahnghong."

From the WMSCOG website:

> "God's name was 'Jehovah' when He played the role of the Father, and it was 'Jesus' when He worked as the Son. Then, how should we call upon God when He is working as the Holy Spirit? The name of the Holy Spirit is Ahnsahnghong."

As stated before, it appears the WMSCOG believes the Bible is the Word of God since it uses the Bible extensively to justify their beliefs in "Christ" Ahnsahnghong and Mother God. But adopting a Modalist view that the Trinity is the same divine person appearing in 3 different forms at three different times, as the WMSCOG does, becomes a huge problem if we accept the Bible as the inerrant Word of God. Why? Quite frankly, it makes God look schizophrenic.

The Schizophrenic God

Schizophrenia literally means "split mind." If Ahnsahnghong is both God the Father and God the Son/Jesus at different times, then who is Jesus praying to in the Garden of Gethsemane?

30

"Abba! Father! All things are possible for You; remove this cup from Me; yet not what I will, but what You will" (Mark 14:36)

In the Garden of Gethsemane, if Ahnsahnghong is Jesus/The Son, how is he praying to The Father? According to the WMSCOG's own theology, when Ahnsahnghong is The Son, then he's no longer The Father. The Father and The Son did not exist at the same time. When Ahnsahnghong was Jesus 2,000 years ago, he was no longer in the form of God the Father, so who is Jesus praying to throughout the Gospels?

Take, for example, Jesus' prayer in **John 17**:

"Jesus spoke these things; and lifting up His eyes to heaven, He said, "Father, the hour has come; glorify Your Son, that the Son may glorify You, even as You gave Him authority over all flesh, that to all whom You have given Him, He may give eternal life...

"I do not ask on behalf of these alone, but for those also who believe in Me through their word; that they may all be one; even as You, Father, are in Me and I in You, that they also may be in Us, so that the world may believe that You sent Me...

"O righteous Father, although the world has not known You, yet I have known You; and these have known that You sent Me; and I have made Your name known to them..."

So, who is Ahnsahnghong talking to? Himself? Let's do an experiment: Let's replace all of the references to God the Son/Jesus, God the Father, and all pronouns for both of them with Ahnsahnghong's name and see how that works out…

"Ahnsahnghong spoke these things; and lifting up His eyes to heaven, He said, "Ahnsahnghong, the hour has come; glorify Ahnsahnghong, that Ahnsahnghong may glorify Ahnsahnghong, even as Ahnsahnghong gave Ahnsahnghong authority over all flesh, that to all whom Ahnsahnghong have given Ahnsahnghong, Ahnsahnghong may give eternal life…

"I, Ahnsahnghong, do not ask on behalf of these alone, but for those also who believe in Ahnsahnghong through their word; that they may all be one; even as You, Ahnsahnghong, are in Ahnsahnghong, and Ahnsahnghong in Ahnsahnghong that they also may be in Us (Ahnsahnghong and Ahnsahnghong), so that the world may believe that Ahnsahnghong sent Ahnsahnghong …

"O righteous Ahnsahnghong, although the world has not known Ahnsahnghong, yet Ahnsahnghong has known Ahnsahnghong; and these have known that Ahnsahnghong sent Ahnsahnghong; and Ahnsahnghong has made Ahnsahnghong's name known to them…"

See what I mean by schizophrenic?

Furthermore, I'd like to know what the WMSCOG makes of **Matthew 3:16-17,** Jesus' baptism by John the Baptist:

"After being baptized, Jesus came up immediately from the water; and behold, the heavens were

32

opened, and he saw the Spirit of God descending as a dove and lighting on Him, and behold, a voice out of the heavens said, 'This is My beloved Son, in whom I am well-pleased.'"

Here, we clearly see the complete Trinity all acting at the same moment in time: Jesus (God the Son) is being baptized. God the Holy Spirit descends to him. And God the Father speaks from heaven.

This single passage destroys the Modalist view, and thus, the WMSCOG's view of the Trinity.

And So...

If the WMSCOG's explanation of the Trinity (the Modalist view) is correct, then the WMSCOG has to give up on the Bible as the inerrant Word of God or accept a schizophrenic view of God.

The WMSCOG clearly gets it wrong when it comes to the Trinity and all things concerning Ahnsahnghong as divine.

Please understand that my effort to expose and discredit the World Mission Society Church of God is not out of malice, spite, or because I have nothing else better to do. I am concerned for those led astray by Ahnsahnghong.

The good news is Jesus Christ, the true Savior, gives new starts and new lives. No one is beyond Jesus Christ's salvation, even sinners like you and me, who are made in God's image and have eternal worth to him.

CHAPTER 5

Mother God & Genesis 1

"The World Mission Society Church of God believes in God the Mother," their website proudly proclaims.

Before I knew anything else about the WMSCOG, including the true name of their church, I had heard from a few friends about being approached by a "cult" talking about "Mother God."

(Again, it's not my intent here to accuse the WMSCOG of being a "cult" or to debate whether it is a cult or not, but to analyze their use of the Bible.)

This chapter and the remaining chapters will analyze what the WMSCOG is most known for: their belief in God the Mother (who currently lives in the flesh in South Korea).

As before, I've purposely avoided exposing myself to any negative websites or information about the WMSCOG and have based my analysis strictly on their explanation of their own beliefs a stated on their official website (http://usa.watv.org/). Since the WMSCOG uses the Bible to explain and defend their views (and they appear to believe the Bible is the Word of God), I will continue to use the Bible to analyze their beliefs.

Mother God – The Evidence

So, where does the WMSCOG get this idea that "Mother God" exists? Most people who know anything about the Bible would be astonished (to say the least) to learn that the Bible, according to the WMSCOG, actually teaches about Mother God.

As you will see, if these verses are the best evidence the WMSCOG has for a biblical teaching of Mother God, their faith is based on a brittle foundation. The first verse, Genesis 1:26-27, is perhaps the most quoted and the most troublesome, so we'll start there:

Genesis 1:26-27:

"Then God said, 'Let Us make man in Our image, according to Our likeness; and let them rule over the fish of the sea and over the birds of the sky and over the cattle and over all the earth, and over every creeping thing that creeps on the earth.' God created man in His own image, in the image of God He created him; male and female He created them."

In Genesis 1:26-27, God creates man and woman in his image. The WMSCOG focuses on the plural language God uses to refer to himself: "us" and "our." Furthermore, they are correct in that in this passage the word "Elohim," which is translated from the original Hebrew into English as "God," is also in the plural form.

According to the teachings of the WMSCOG, since "the principle of nature" is that both male and female are

35

needed to create life, and since God made both man and woman in his image, there must be both a male (Father) and female (Mother) God. The site claims "us" and "our" is often interpreted as referring to the Trinity (God the Father, God the Son, and God the Holy Spirit), but this is incorrect; it can't be the Trinity, says the WMSCOG, because then three types of people would exist in the world today, not two: male and female.

Thus, in the creation story at the beginning of the Bible, we have evidence of Mother God.

The WMSCOG also cites **Isaiah 6:8** to show the plurality of God:

"Then I heard the voice of the Lord, saying, 'Whom shall I send, and who will go for Us?' Then I [Isaiah] said, 'Here am I. Send me!'"

God or Gods?

As said above, this is the most troublesome passage used by the WMSCOG, but I only say that because it's a difficult passage for anyone studying the Bible because it does contain some unusual grammatical features and needs more explanation than the other passages they use. Churches with unusual, unorthodox beliefs often snatch challenging passages to justify their more peculiar beliefs.

Interestingly, the first time I came across anyone who pointed out the use of plural words (Elohim, us, our) in Genesis 1:26-27 was when I was in my early twenties in an Introduction to the Bible class in college. The professor was either a former pastor or priest (I can't remember which) who had evidently lost his faith. Even though I was atheistic/agnostic at the time and I was eating up much of what he was teaching, even then he came across to me as quite hostile towards the Bible and anyone who had a more traditional view of it.

Liberal and skeptical biblical scholars who don't believe the first book of the Bible was written by Moses and inspired by God but instead was a Frankenstein-like combination of various writings from the ancient world, grab on to Genesis 1:26-27 to support their views. These scholars seize on the plural words as evidence that the Jewish religion – an ardent monotheistic religion – actually originated from polytheistic religions. The most prominent theory from these liberal Bible scholars says that four earlier sources from different cultures contributed to the formation of Genesis as we know it today.

We won't go into it here, but conservative biblical scholars have contested these claims. The biggest stumbling block for the liberal scholars' view is that there is no hard evidence, such as manuscript proof, to support their theory. Further, I think a simple question pokes rather large holes in their theory: If Genesis is a mixing of religious texts from polytheistic cultures and the early Jews edited them into the first book of the Bible to create a vehemently monotheistic religion, why and how did they overlook the very obvious polytheistic plural words? Why didn't they just change them?

5 (Much More Likely) Alternatives to the Mother God Interpretation

Now, moving on from liberal biblical scholarship to the claims of the WMSCOG concerning Genesis 1:26-27 and Mother God: What *is* the deal with the plural language? Jewish, Christian, and secular scholars have offered several explanations:

(1) God is addressing his "heavenly court," the angels.

Many Jewish commentators, some dating back to ancient times like Philo of Alexandria, uphold this view. See the following passages as biblical evidence of the heavenly court: Job 1; Psalm 89:6-8; 1 Kings 22:19-22; Daniel 7:9-13; Luke 2:9-14; and Revelation 4-5. In Isaiah 6:8 ("who will go for Us?"), the idea that God is speaking to a heavenly court appears to be the clear case when the verse is read in context with the rest of Isaiah 6.

(2) God is addressing the rest of the Trinity.

Though from a Christian perspective there is a possibility that the Holy Spirit moved Moses to include this reference to the Trinity in the first book of the Bible, even conservative Christian scholars agree that this interpretation is unlikely. Though possible, the idea is wholly speculative, and it's highly unlikely the original author, Moses, consciously made reference to the Trinity.

(3) God is addressing other gods.

Is the plural language evidence that Judaism grew out of a polytheistic culture? I addressed some of the issues with this theory above. Commentators point out that the radically monotheistic Jews would've never included such polytheistic language.

(4) God is using the "plural of majesty."

Like how English royalty will say "we" when speaking since royalty speaks for the whole kingdom, God as creator of all things is using plural pronouns (us, our) in relation to his supremely eminent position. Though we see one example of this in the Bible in Ezra 4:18, this view is widely rejected because we simply do not see plural pronouns used in the Hebrew language this way anywhere else, whether inside or outside the Bible. (But we'll return to this idea later when speaking about the plural "Elohim.")

(5) God is self-deliberating and/or self-addressing.

Basically, the idea is God is talking to himself – as if thinking aloud. This simple explanation is the most widely accepted, and as one commentator writes, the idea is "an attested and sufficient explanation," as it is well supported by other examples in the Hebrew language where the language shifts between plural and singular.

An example of a human being doing this is in **2 Samuel 24:14**:

"Then David said to Gad, 'I am in great distress. Let <u>us</u> fall into the hand of the Lord, for his mercy is great; but let me not fall into the hand of man.'"

An example where God does this is in **Genesis 11:6-8** during the Tower of Babel episode:

"And the LORD said, 'Behold, they are one people, and they have all one language, and this is only the beginning of what they will do. And nothing that they propose to do will now be impossible for them. Come, let <u>us</u> go down and there confuse their language, so that they may not understand one another's speech.' So the LORD dispersed them from there over the face of all the earth, and they left off building the city."

Notice "the LORD" says, "let us go down," but then we're immediately told "the LORD dispersed them." Here, in the original Hebrew, "the LORD" is not the plural Elohim (a general title for God) but "Yahwah," God's name as given to Moses. (More about this below.) Yahwah, being God's unique name, can only be taken as referring to a singular being, yet we also see the plural pronoun "us" used. Clearly, there are not two or more gods involved here, but only the one true God, Yahweh.

So, to say here we see a plurality of gods because of the use of "us" is nonsensical; we have to understand "us" as a language device of the ancient Hebrews. To say otherwise would be the equivalent of saying the following statements means that Frank is more than one person: *"Let us eat some dinner," said Frank. So, Frank ate some dinner.*

Likewise, though the "us" in Isaiah 6:8 may be addressing the heavenly court, it may be another example of God's self-deliberation as in Genesis 11:6-8. Notice how the language shifts between singular and plural in Isaiah 6:8:

Then I heard the voice of the Lord [singular], saying, "Whom shall I [singular] send, and who will go for us [plural]?"

If we don't want to accept either explanation that God is self-deliberating or speaking to the angels, then we have to conclude God or the writers of the Old Testament were really bad at Hebrew grammar, not knowing the difference between singular and plural pronouns! But the one thing that certainly can't be logically concluded by this is that God is speaking to another god, let alone God the Mother.

In Hebrew, Even Verbs Are Plural

To hammer home this point even more, the original Hebrew of Genesis 1:26-27 uses singular forms of verbs in these passages even though plural pronouns are used. Obviously, this doesn't translate into English since English doesn't have singular and plural forms of verbs. If Genesis 1:26-27 shows Father God and Mother God speaking, why would the verbs be singular?

Thus, the explanation of God's self-deliberation is the most likely explanation for Genesis 1:26-27 because had God been speaking to others in these plural instances – such as to a heavenly court or another deity like Mother God – the verbs surrounding the statements would be plural.

The "Names" of God

For clarity's sake (and simply because this is good to know), there are three words in the Bible regularly used to refer to God:

Hebrew translated to English		
Elohim	**=**	**God (title)**
Yahweh	**=**	**the LORD (God's name)**
Adonai	**=**	**the Lord (title)**

Yahweh – When you see the "LORD" in all caps in your English-language Bible, the original Hebrew reads "*Yahweh*," the name of the one true God as given to Moses in Exodus 3:14 ("Yahweh" means "I AM").

Elohim – *Elohim* (or El, Elah, or Elo'ah – These are the singular forms) is a general title translated "God" when referring to the one true God, Yahweh, but it can refer to false gods and other powerful beings (such as angels) or even powerful people. (For example, see Psalm 82:1-6 and Jesus' reference to it in John 10:34–36). Though this word doesn't exclusively mean the one true God, it is obvious by the context when it is referring to Yahweh.

42

Adonai – Similarly, *Adonai* is a general title and can refer to a human master or lord. Again, we must look at the context the word is used in to know if it is referring to God. (Also, keep in mind, there is no capitalization in Hebrew.)

"Lord GOD" – Sometimes we see *Adonai* and *Yahweh* together, so it's translated "Lord GOD." (Note the use of caps in the English translation.)

Elohim = God's "Otherness"

So, we explained the plural pronouns, but what's the deal with "Elohim" – the actual word translated "God" – being plural?

The use of the plural Elohim in Hebrew suggests God's unique nature as the one and only immaterial, timeless, self-sufficiently existent and powerful creator of all things. This can be closest understood in human terms as the "plurality of royalty," such as the Queen of England would use, we discussed above.

God's "otherness" – meaning his uniqueness in absolute supremacy, majesty, and holiness – from all other things is a regular theme in the Bible, as the Jews understood God was wholly "other." The plural Elohim illustrates this.

The Baker Encyclopedia explains Elohim "is plural in form, but when applied to the true God it is used in a singular sense… The most common explanation for the plural form of Elohim as applied to God is that it is 'plural of majesty,' that is, all the majesty of deity is encompassed by him."

Likewise, God's self-proclaimed name as given to Moses in **Exodus 3:13-14** is all about his exclusive, one-of-a-kind nature:

Then Moses said to God, "Behold, I am going to the sons of Israel, and I will say to them, 'The God of your fathers has sent me to you.' Now they may say to me, 'What is His name?' What shall I say to them?" God said to Moses, "I AM WHO I AM"; and He said, "Thus you shall say to the sons of Israel, 'I AM has sent me to you.'"

What an awesome statement by God! Essentially, God isn't giving a name but an explanation of his being. Since there's no worldly thing to compare him to – and he is beyond any comparison – God simply states, "I AM WHO I AM." In other words: I am self-existent and self-sufficient; I am the Uncaused First Cause; I am the only Necessary Being; and there is nothing else like me. In Hebrew, "I AM" is "Yahweh." (Hebrew doesn't have vowels, so it's literally "YHWH.") Both "I AM" and "Elohim" emphasize what the Jews knew very well: God is utterly "other."

The New American Commentary speaks of the use of Elohim instead of Yahweh in the creation story:

"The general name Elohim is appropriate for the creation account's universal framework and in effect repudiates the cosmogonies of the pagan world, where the origins and biography of their 'gods' are paramount. From the inception of [the first 5 books of the Bible] polytheism and idolatry have no ideological or practical place among Israel." (See Exodus 20:1-6; Deut. 4:12-24.)

44

One blogger explains it particularly well:

"When used of the true God, 'Elohim' denotes what is called by linguists a plural of majesty, honor, or fullness. That is, he is GOD in the fullest sense of the word. He is 'GOD of gods' or literally, 'ELOHIM of elohim.'" (See Deut. 10:17; Psalm 136:2.)

Not Convinced? How About Masculine, Singular Pronouns?

Even if you don't find the explanations I've offered here convincing, and even if you reject all of the interpretations listed above, all of the above is still much more plausible and logical than the conclusions of the WMSCOG. Yes, Genesis 1:26-27 uses the plural form Elohim; yes, God sometimes uses plural personal pronouns; yes, God made man and woman in his image. But it's a huge jump in logic to say these verses serve as evidence of Mother God. Clearly, this conclusion can only be reached if preconceived ideas are read into the verses, not by letting the Bible speak for itself.

Let's also note that **Genesis 1:27** plainly states:

"God created man in <u>His</u> own image, in the image of God <u>He</u> created him; male and female <u>He</u> created them."

45

Yes, in the original Hebrew those are *masculine, singular pronouns*. It does not say:

God created man in <u>Their</u> own image, in the image of God <u>They</u> created him; male and female <u>They</u> created them.

And though we know the immaterial God is not male in a physical sense, the masculine pronoun is clearly used. If the WMSCOG's theory that since there are two types of people, male and female, there must be male and female Gods is correct, then Genesis 1:27 would read something like this:

God created man in His own image, in the image of God He created him; male He created him. And God created woman in Her own image, in the image of God She created her; female she created her.

In fact, if we're going to go in this direction, why doesn't Genesis 1 just plainly state that Father God and Mother God created humankind together? Clearly, Genesis doesn't say this because I AM doesn't need a female partner to create. Yes, God created the world so that much of his physical creation does need both male and female to procreate, but the self-existent, all-powerful I AM is not a physical being. He made humankind (and everything) from nothing. The great I AM is not restricted by the physical world; he created the physical world. He is wholly "other."

And so...

One has to question why literally thousands of years of Jewish, Christian, and (much of it hostile) secular tradition and scholarship has never discovered Mother God in the Bible before.

But let's keep an open mind: Yes, I believe this chapter refutes the most widely quoted passage by the WMSCOG to justify their belief in Mother God, and as I said above, it is probably the most difficult to explain due to the perceived oddity of the grammar since none of us are ancient Hebrews. But still I'll keep an open mind and do what I always do when someone offers an interpretation of the Bible that doesn't seem quite right to me:

I ask for more evidence.

Certainly, there has to be more evidence of Mother God in God's Word than one (fairly easily refuted) passage at the very beginning of the Bible, right?

In the following chapters, we'll look at other verses the WMSCOG claims speak about Mother God.

CHAPTER 6

Mother God & Jeremiah 31

The World Mission Society Church of God believes "Mother God" not only exists in the flesh today in South Korea, but she exists in the Bible.

In the previous chapter we analyzed the WMSCOG 's use of Genesis 1:26-27 and Isaiah 6:8 to justify their belief in Mother God. Below, we'll continue to analyze the Scripture they cite as biblical proof of Mother God.

As stated earlier, since the WMSCOG uses the Bible to defend their views (and they appear to believe the Bible is the Word of God), I've used the Bible to analyze and refute their beliefs as unbiblical and as a corruption of the true Gospel of Jesus Christ.

The following practices of poor biblical interpretation (manipulation-?) are the most evident in the WMSCOG's use of Scripture:

- **Isolating verses and taking them out of context.**

- **Imposing views on the text rather than letting the text speak for itself.**

- **Jumping from one part of the Bible to another with utter disregard of context to "prove" ideas, beliefs, or opinions.**

- **Inconsistent decisions on what should be taken literally or figuratively, often based on preconceived ideas.**

*Now may be a good time to pause and review Chapter 2 about proper (and poor) biblical interpretation.

Jeremiah 31:22:

"How long will you go here and there,

O faithless daughter?

For the Lord has created a new thing in the earth—

A woman will encompass a man."

Like many of the passages the WMSCOG cites as evidence of Mother God in the Bible, Jeremiah 31:22 sounds mysterious, and may even lead you to suspect there is some sort of hidden meaning behind it, but by simply looking at the verse in context, the meaning of the passage becomes clear.

Context, Context, Context

The prophet Jeremiah wrote his book during the harsh, tumultuous times after the rise of the Babylonian Empire, after the destruction of Jerusalem and the Jewish temple, and after the deportation (the Exile) of Jews from their homeland to Babylon. Like the other prophets, Jeremiah states God allowed this calamity to fall on the Jewish people as just judgment for their sin and idolatry

But, also like the other prophets, Jeremiah isn't all gloom and bad news: he also gives a message of hope, where God will redeem the faithful.

This message of hope is seen in the verses preceding Jeremiah 31:22. Take a moment to read it, covering at least 31:15 to 31:22.

Rachel is Weeping

In verse 31:15, we find reference to Rachel, who is weeping for "her children," the exiled Jews:

"Rachel is weeping for her children;

she refuses to be comforted for her children,

because they are no more."

Who is Rachel? We find Rachel way back in the book of Genesis, the first book of the Bible. Rachel was Jacob's second, but favorite, wife (Genesis 29:30) and the mother of Joseph, the father of Ephraim and Manasseh (Genesis 30:22-24; 41:50-52). Notice Ephraim is mentioned in Jeremiah 31:18 as also grieving.

Like many of the prophets, Jeremiah uses a lot of poetic imagery. The idea here is that the Exile is so devastating to the Jews that even Rachel is mourning. It would be similar if I said to an American today, after someone had burned an American flag, that Betsy Ross (the woman traditionally credited with sewing the 1st American flag) is weeping over the treatment of the flag. The person would know that I didn't mean this literally, since Betsy Ross lived in the 1700-1800's, but poetically.

But Jeremiah moves on to the good news. God will have mercy, and a faithful remnant will return to their homeland. Note the imagery of roads in 31:21, implying their return:

"Set up road markers for yourself;

make yourself guideposts;

consider well the highway,

the road by which you went."

Israel, the Jewish people, are then poetically personified as a young woman, a "virgin" and "faithless daughter" in 31:21-22:

"Return, O virgin Israel,

return to these your cities.

How long will you waver,

O faithless daughter?"

51

And then we have the mysterious and infamous words of 31:22, used by the WMSCOG as evidence of Mother God:

"For the Lord has created a new thing on the earth:

a woman encircles a man."

First, it's clear from the context of the rest of Jeremiah that jumping to the conclusion that this verse is about a female deity of any sort has no textual or logical grounding. If you continue to read the rest of Jeremiah, you will find so such evidence of "Mother God" either.

Admittedly, this single line "a woman encircles a man" is a bit of a mystery. One commentator even says the clear meaning of this line is "enigmatic." Yet the only way to justify that this is about Mother God is to read a preconceived idea into the text, not by letting the text speak for itself. Furthermore, even if the statement is unclear, the woman in the verse is clearly Israel.

Unorthodox sects and cults often grab onto unclear lines of Scripture and insert their own meaning into them. Interestingly, the same commentator who labeled this line "enigmatic" also writes that though this one line is unclear, the rest of the chapter surrounding it is perfectly clear and unambiguous.

Though Israel is a "faithless daughter," God will still give her a "new thing" – a new life as he brings her back to her homeland from exile. "Encircles" in 31:22 ("a woman encircles a man") can also be translated "encompasses" or "protects." What the line is most likely symbolizing is that the "woman" (Israel) will grow in strength, even to the point of being strong enough to protect "a man."

As you can see, nothing in Jeremiah supports the claim that Mother God appears in this ancient book of prophecy.

CHAPTER 7

Mother God & Galatians 4

"But the Jerusalem above is free, and she is our mother." (Galatians 4:26)

"So, brothers, we are not children of the slave but of the free woman." (Galatians 4:31)

Above are two verses from the Bible (Galatians 4:26 & 4:31) that the WMSCOG quotes on their website as evidence for Mother God in the Bible. Now, you may be thinking Galatians 4:26 even mentions the word "mother," so it must be about Mother God! But let's look at what Paul is writing about in Galatians.

Remember context is always the key.

What's Paul So Angry About?

Galatians is considered Paul's most angry letter. It even excludes Paul's normal thanksgiving in his opening introduction for those receiving the letter. Its absence is very noticeable because we see similar friendly openings in all of his other letters – even the more stern ones. So what's Paul so upset about?

The Galatians had reverted back to legalism, believing that Christians must still follow the Jewish religious laws for salvation. This was a big issue with the first Christians because Christianity came out of Judaism, the first

54

Christians were Jews, and ancient Jews faithfully followed the Old Testament law.

But Christians have been set free from the law because Jesus Christ fulfilled it by his death and resurrection. The religious law was temporary until the good news of Christ came and freed us from it (See Galatians 3:15-25).

The Christians in Galatia had backslid and had gone back to believing (and teaching) that everyone must still follow the Old Testament religious laws, even as saved Christians (See Galatians 4:8-20).

Paul spent a lot of time proclaiming that Christian salvation was not gained through works (whether religious rituals or good deeds) but through faith in Christ and God's grace alone. When we come to Galatians 4:21-31, Paul uses a story from the book of Genesis about Abraham's wives Hagar and Sarah and their sons to illustrate his point. The idea Paul is arguing is that someone can choose to be a slave to the Old Testament law or free through Christ, but one cannot be both.

Abraham & his Wives = Domestic Trouble

Abraham (Abram) is the father of the Israelite nation, the Jews. In Genesis 12:1-3, God speaks to Abraham and promises him that he will make a great nation through Abraham's descendants, through which the whole world will be blessed. (This promise was fulfilled with the coming of the Messiah, Jesus Christ, a descendant of Abraham.)

But later, in Chapter 15, Abraham and his wife Sarah (Sarai) still do not have a single child. God reaffirms his promise, telling Abraham that his descendants will be as numerous as the stars in the sky (Genesis 15:5).

In Chapter 16, we get the story of Sarah (Sarai) and Hagar. Sarah has grown weary of waiting for God to give them a child, so she tells Abraham to sleep with their servant/slave Hagar. Abraham listens to his wife, and Hagar becomes pregnant and gives birth to Ishmael.

This was sinful for both Abraham and Sarah. Beyond the obvious sexual sin, both Abraham and Sarah didn't trust God to fulfill his promise and they took matters into their own hands. As you can imagine, the situation also leads to domestic trouble.

Fourteen years later, in Chapter 21, Abraham is one hundred years old, and Sarah is in her nineties, and as God promised, Sarah becomes pregnant! She gives birth to Isaac. Again, as you can probably guess, the birth of Isaac doesn't help the domestic situation.

Sarah witnesses Ishmael, now a teen, mocking either her or Isaac, so Hagar and Ishmael are cast out of the home of Abraham. Though Ishmael wouldn't receive an inheritance from his father Abraham, God cares for him and his mother and promises that Ishmael's descendants would become a great nation as well.

The Free Woman & The Slave Woman

Now, back to Galatians 4:21-31: Paul uses Sarah (the free woman) and Hagar (the slave woman) to make a point about being free through Jesus Christ or a slave to the Old Testament law. (Take a moment to read Galatians 4:21-31.)

First, let's take note that Paul clearly states in 4:24 that he's using the story as an *allegory*, a symbolic tale to convey a message:

"Now this may be interpreted allegorically: these women are two covenants."

Thus, he's clearly speaking figuratively here, not literally.

Basically, Paul's whole analogy in 4:21-31 goes like this: God gave two covenants — one of slavery and one of freedom, symbolized by Sarah (the free woman) and Hagar (the slave woman).

Paul writes:

"One is from Mount Sinai, bearing children for slavery; she is Hagar. Now Hagar is Mount Sinai in Arabia; she corresponds to the present Jerusalem, for she is in slavery with her children." (4:24-25)

The covenant of slavery is the Old Testament law, represented by Hagar and Mount Sinai (the place where Moses received the Old Testament law from God). This covenant of slavery is also represented by the "present Jerusalem" – the non-Christian Jews of Paul's day who have rejected Jesus Christ and still follow the Old Testament religious laws. They are the "children" of the slave woman because the Old Testament law enslaves them.

Paul then writes the line used by the WMSCOG:

"But the Jerusalem above is free, and she is our mother." (4:26)

Following Paul's analogy and argument, "Jerusalem above" is contrasted with the present, worldly Jerusalem, which is still in bondage to the Old Testament law. "Jerusalem above" is the heavenly Jerusalem – the true, free Jerusalem. This looks forward – past the present age to the future – to the New Heaven and New Earth where the New Jerusalem will come with Jesus' Second Coming (See Revelation 21)(More about this next chapter also). Keeping with the Hagar/Sarah (slave woman/free woman) analogy, Paul states in 4:26 that the New Jerusalem is the "mother" of Christians because they're not slaves; they are free.

Keeping with the imagery of Sarah (who was old and barren when she became pregnant) and the future victory of Christianity and the New Jerusalem, Paul quotes Isaiah 54:1 in Galatians 4:27:

"Rejoice, O barren one who does not bear;

break forth and cry aloud, you who are not in labor!

For the children of the desolate one will be more

than those of the one who has a husband."

Paul goes on to explain in 4:28-30 that Christians, like Isaac, are the children of God's promise (4:28). And just like

58

Ishmael ("who was born according to the flesh") showed contempt for Isaac (who was "born according to the Spirit") when he was born, the non-believing Jews are persecuting the Christians of Galatia "now" (4:29). Yet — Paul, here, quotes Genesis directly — Ishmael was cast out and didn't get the inheritance of his father Abraham (4:30), implying the same will happen to the Jews who still hold to the Old Testament religious law and don't believe the good news of Jesus Christ.

Thus, Paul concludes with the other line used by the WMSCOG:

"So, brothers, we are not children of the slave but of the free woman." (4:31)

Thus, Christians are not slaves, but free. To be a child of "the slave" would make someone a child of Hagar. Likewise, the "free woman" is not some divine goddess, but Sarah.

This will help you to follow the argument made by Paul:

SLAVERY =

1. **Old Testament law =**
2. **Mount Sinai =**
3. **"Present" Jerusalem =**
4. **Hagar (slave woman) =**
5. **Ishmael =**

No inheritance.

FREEDOM =

1. **Salvation through faith alone =**
2. **Jesus Christ =**
3. **Jerusalem above/New Jerusalem=**
4. **Sarah (free woman) =**
5. **Isaac =**

Receives the inheritance.

CHAPTER 8

Mother God & Revelation

Revelation is a favorite book of the Bible for unorthodox sects, full-blown cults, and a general assortment of crazies because it's highly symbolic and notoriously difficult to understand. Because of this, people can read all sorts of nutty things into the text that simply aren't there.

The WMSCOG uses primarily two passages from Revelation, in chapters 19 and 21, to "prove" Mother God is in the Bible. As always, before looking at these passages, we must first understand the context in which they appear. Understanding cannot come without context, yet often verses are quoted alone by the WMSCOG and other groups that misuse or misinterpret the Bible.

Context: The Grand Climax

The book of Revelation is the last book of the Bible, and Chapters 19 through 22 of Revelation are the absolute last chapters of the Bible. Thus, Chapters 19-22 are the grand climax of the story of salvation recorded in the Bible and, in the Christian worldview, the culmination of all of human history.

Here would be a good time to pause for a short overview of the complete story of the Bible:

Salvation History

Biblical theology is the study of the story of the Bible *as a whole*. The Bible is not a collection of random, disconnected episodes; it tells the story of God's progressive revelation throughout history, often referred to as ***Salvation History*** because the whole purpose of God's work in much of human history is salvation. Few people have an understanding of this, and comprehending this will help a lot of believers and nonbelievers to better understand the Christian faith.

Christians believe the Bible (and history) moves through 4 major events/eras:

(1) Creation — (2) Fall — (3) Redemption — (4) Restoration

At *the Creation*, God made the world good, but mankind (because he was given freewill) sinned and rebelled against God (*the Fall*). All of creation was affected by the Fall, and humankind was forever separated from an eternally good, holy God by their sin. But God chose Israel as his special people and prepared them for the coming of Christ (the Messiah). Christians believe the whole Old Testament is preparing the world for the coming of Christ. (Jewish theologians would agree with this but disagree that Jesus is the Christ.)

Then, Jesus the Christ came, lived the sinless life that none of us could, and died for the sins of the world in our place (*the Redemption*). Being both God and man, only Jesus could accomplish this. This puts into action *the Restoration*; people will be redeemed through faith in Jesus Christ. This is where we are now in history, but the Restoration won't reach fulfillment until Jesus' Second Coming, at which time creation will be made right again.

The phrase **"already/not yet"** is often used to speak of the time period we now live in within history; Jesus Christ has *already* started the Restoration, but the completion of the Restoration has *not yet* arrived.

What About Between the Fall and the Redemption?

Since the Creation and the Fall happened all within only the first 3 chapters of Genesis, and the Redemption doesn't happen until Jesus' life, the majority of the Old Testament tells of the period between the Fall and Redemption, covering about 2,000 years once God appears to Abraham. (It's unclear how much time passes during the earlier events recorded in Genesis to Abraham.) During these 2,000 years, God prepared Israel (and the world) for the Redemption, the coming of the Christ. As I said above, Christians understand all of the Old Testament to point towards Jesus.

So, we're in the Restoration. Now what?

Christians are commanded by Jesus Christ to spread the good news of his sacrificial love so all can be redeemed from sin, to stay strong in their faith and be led by the Holy Spirit, and to wait. Wait for what? Jesus Christ's Second Coming, when he will complete the Restoration with the Final Judgment and usher in the New Heavens and New Earth. The final destination of people who aren't separated from God by sin will not be heaven, but the restored earth. Moreover, no new revelations from God, including new scriptures, are coming or are needed.

This is traditional, biblical Christianity.

Revelation 19-22: The Final Victory

Chapters 19-22 of the Book of Revelation closes the Bible and foretells the completion of the Restoration – the final, ultimate victory of Jesus Christ, God the Son. In these chapters, the "multitude" in heaven rejoices as Christ returns to live in peace with his creation. But first the returning Christ must carry out the Final Judgment and the defeat of his enemies — evil, sin, Satan, and death (in easily the most gory and violent verses of the whole Bible). Afterwards, the old creation, which was corrupted by sin, passes away, and the New Heaven and New Earth come, where God the Son will live with his people eternally in peace.

*Now would be a good time to pause and read Revelation 19-22.

Marriage Imagery

The first verse the WMSCOG uses from Revelation is:

Revelation 19:7:

*"Let us rejoice and exult
and give him the glory,
for the marriage of the Lamb has come,
and his Bride has made herself ready;"*

Based on symbolic language used throughout the New Testament, including Revelation, the Lamb is clearly Jesus Christ. Since the WMSCOG agrees here with orthodox Christianity and this interpretation is uncontroversial, there's no need to discuss the Lamb imagery further here. But "his Bride" is not Mother God, as the WMSCOG believes, but the church.

Throughout the New Testament, Jesus is often referred to as a bridegroom (or "groom," in modern terms) and the church – the united community of Jesus' followers – is often referred to as his "bride." Though Revelation contains a lot of baffling symbolism, this symbolism is extremely clear due to its wide use.

For example, in **Mark 2:19**, Jesus refers to himself as the bridegroom:

"And Jesus said to them, 'Can the wedding guests fast while the bridegroom is with them? As long as they have the bridegroom with them, they cannot fast.'"

In **John 3:29**, John the Baptist also describes Jesus as the bridegroom:

"The one who has the bride is the bridegroom. The friend of the bridegroom, who stands and hears him, rejoices greatly at the bridegroom's voice. Therefore this joy of mine is now complete."

Further, in **2 Corinthians 11:2**, Paul uses marriage imagery. The Corinthian church is being led astray from the truth of Christ, but Paul says he has married them to Christ, the church's "husband," as if they were pure virgins.

"For I feel a divine jealousy for you, since I betrothed you to one husband, to present you as a pure virgin to Christ."

Likewise, in Ephesians 5:22-33, the love of a husband and wife is compared to the love of Christ for his church. Just as a husband and wife join lives and become "one flesh," Christ and the church become one flesh. In fact, God created marriage to symbolize Christ's relationship to the church.

For instance, **Ephesians 5:25-27** reads:

"Husbands, love your wives, as Christ loved the church and gave himself up for her, that he might sanctify her, having cleansed her by the washing of water with the word, so that he might present the church to himself in splendor, without spot or wrinkle or any such thing, that she might be holy and without blemish."

And if that evidence doesn't convince you, in **Matthew 22:1-14** Jesus tells a parable about a wedding feast to describe his coming kingdom. (Take a moment to read it right now.)

Appropriately, when Revelation 19-21 tells us of the ultimate culmination of God's kingdom, what sort of imagery does the writer use? Wedding imagery!

Further, this imagery is not unique to the New Testament. Like much of the imagery used in the New Testament — and especially Revelation — it goes back to the Old Testament. For example, **Isaiah 25:6-8** uses imagery of a celebration feast to describe the age-to-come under God's victory and complete, perfect rule:

"On this mountain the Lord of hosts will make for all peoples
a feast of rich food, a feast of well-aged wine,
of rich food full of marrow, of aged wine well refined."

In fact, notice the similar language in **Isaiah 25:8** and **Revelation 21:4**, proving a further connection between these two passages about God's future victory and coming kingdom:

"He will swallow up death forever;
and the Lord God will wipe away tears from all faces..." (Isaiah 25:8)

"He will wipe away every tear from their eyes, and death shall be no more, neither shall there be mourning, nor crying, nor pain anymore, for the former things have passed away." (Revelation 21:4)

(*Since it is so common for unorthodox churches to take verses out of context to "prove" their misguided interpretations, again I encourage you to read all quoted Scripture in context so you can see that I am representing the Bible accurately.)

In fact, marriage language is used throughout the Old Testament to describe God's relationship to Israel, his chosen people. Israel is often portrayed as the bride of God, and likewise, often accused of adultery for being unfaithful to God.

All of these marriage images are important to what's going on in Chapters 19-22 of Revelation, which describes Jesus' Second Coming — bringing with him the New Heaven and New Earth, which is the culmination of God's kingdom and the final, perfect union of Christ and his people, the church.

Earlier in Revelation, we already see this imagery in **Revelation 14:4**, where the church (Christ's people) are depicted as pure virgins, who have remained faithful to Christ, and are, thus, ready to be wed:

"It is these who have not defiled themselves with women, for they are virgins. It is these who follow the Lamb wherever he goes. These have been redeemed from mankind as firstfruits for God and the Lamb"

Thus, when Jesus returns, it's announced in **Revelation 19:7** that the church, the Bride, is deemed ready for her "marriage" to the Lamb of God, Jesus:

"for the marriage of the Lamb has come, and his Bride has made herself ready;"

Therefore, it's quite obvious the Bride is not any sort of divine goddess, but the church. Revelation tells of the final climatic union of Christ with his church, and the writers of God's Word chose to use the earthly language of marriage to illustrate this joyous day.

New Jerusalem: City or Woman?

The other passage from Revelation used by the WMSCOG is found after Christ's victory over evil and death and at the coming of the New Heaven and New Earth, where Christ comes to live in eternal peace with his people and his renewed creation:

Revelation 21:9-10:

"Then came one of the seven angels who had the seven bowls full of the seven last plagues and spoke to me, saying, 'Come, I will show you the Bride, the wife of the Lamb.' And he carried me away in the Spirit to a great, high mountain, and showed me the holy city Jerusalem coming down out of heaven from God,"

The WMSCOG also calls Mother God "Jerusalem Mother" because in order for what's written in Revelation to work in favor of the WMSCOG's mistaken theology,

69

Jerusalem must be understood to be not a city, but a divine woman, Mother God.

The WMSCOG uses similar thinking in interpreting Galatians 4:26 ("But the Jerusalem above is free, and she is our mother"), but we refuted this in the previous chapter.

This is an odd interpretation to say the least. As with the other verses we analyzed in earlier chapters, there's nothing in Revelation that leads us to conclude that Mother God is a biblical figure or that Jerusalem symbolizes a divine goddess. The only way these interpretations work is if we start with an assumption — an already established idea — of Mother God and insert her into the text.

The "Bride" of Revelation 21:9-10 is not a divine female person to be literally wed to God. The "Bride" is the New Jerusalem, the holy city of the New Earth, where Jesus will spend eternity with his church, his people.

Just before 21:9-10, in **Revelation 21:3-4**, we are given a description of the culmination of God's redemption of creation — the climax of all of Salvation History and the climax of the whole Bible: the coming of the New Heaven and New Earth. All of creation is made new; sin, evil, and death have been destroyed; and God can finally live in perfect shalom with his people.

Revelation 21:3-4 reads:

"And I heard a loud voice from the throne saying, 'Behold, the dwelling place of God is with man. He will dwell with them, and they will be his people, and God himself will be with them as their God. He will wipe away every tear from their eyes, and death shall be no more, neither shall there be

70

mourning, nor crying, nor pain anymore, for the former things have passed away.'"

Revelation is highly symbolic, so how literally we should take the description of the New Jerusalem that follows is debatable, but it's clear we are dealing with a place here — not a person — a place where God will dwell with humankind. New Jerusalem is certainly not a female deity marrying Jesus. In fact, just before 21:9-10, John, the author of Revelation, writes:

"And I saw the holy city, new Jerusalem, coming down out of heaven from God, prepared as a bride adorned for her husband." (21:2)

Here, New Jerusalem is plainly called a "holy city." Further, it's described as being "prepared as a bride." The city is not called a literal bride. The use of "like" or "as" in a comparison shows it's a simile; it's figurative language, not literal language. New Jerusalem is to be the dwelling place of God with his people. Were it to be the other way around, where the bride was to be understood literally and the city was figurative, it would read:

"And I saw the bride, new Jerusalem, coming down out of heaven from God, prepared as a holy city adorned for her husband"

But that doesn't quite work, does it? In fact, why confuse everyone by naming the bride after a city in the first place? Why not just call her Mother God if that is who the bride is?

71

As Craig Blomberg in *From Pentecost to Patmos* writes,

> "...a holy city will descend from the new
> heaven to adorn the new earth. Whereas
> we began in a garden, we will end in a
> city — God's people in perfect
> community. That the city is called the
> new Jerusalem suggests the fulfillment of
> all the promises to Israel as well as to
> humanity in this revelation. But the city
> is also a bride (just as Yahwah [God] and
> Christ are portrayed as bridegrooms to
> their followers throughout the Old and
> New Testaments, respectively.)"

When we come to **Revelation 21:9-10**, the verses the
WMSCOG uses, the "Bride, the wife of the Lamb" is still
referring to the city:

> *"'Come, I will show you the Bride, the wife of the
> Lamb.' And he carried me away in the Spirit to a
> great, high mountain, and showed me the holy city
> Jerusalem coming down out of heaven from God,"*

We are told right in the text that he is shown *a city* as "the
Bride," and what follows after 21:10 is a long description of
that city. If Jerusalem is, in fact, Mother God, aka
"Jerusalem Mother," then she's a divine woman with a
high wall, twelve gates, and the length, width, and height of
1,380 miles; in fact, she is a perfect (and quite humongous)
cube!

72

Now, someone may challenge me and say I admitted above that Revelation is highly symbolic so it's difficult to know what should be taken literally and what should be taken figuratively. Could the description of the New Jerusalem be poetically describing the splendor of Mother God?

As I showed above from the context, we can be confident that we're dealing with a *place* here, not a person. Further, as I've stated many times before, nothing in the Bible gives any indication of a divine mate for God, whether it's referring to Jerusalem or anything else. There simply isn't any evidence. If we accept that the description of New Jerusalem in Revelation is Mother God, then what prevents us from also concluding – despite the obvious lack of evidence – that New Jerusalem symbolizes Darth Vader, George W. Bush, or the NY Jets?

<u>CONCLUSION</u>

As one video on the WMSCOG's website proclaims, the "mystery of the Bible hidden for 6,000 years" has been revealed at last!

Here's a wise rule of thumb: If anyone claims to have a new understanding of the Bible that has never appeared before in the over 2,000 years of history since Jesus walked the earth, be suspicious – be very suspicious.

We would do well to take seriously the warnings of Scripture:

"but test everything; hold fast what is good." (1 Thessalonians 5:21)

"Beloved, do not believe every spirit, but test the spirits to see whether they are from God, for many false prophets have gone out into the world." (1 John 4:1)

And how do we test all things, especially teachings claiming to be from God? We test them against God's own words:

"All Scripture is breathed out by God and profitable for teaching, for reproof, for correction, and for training in righteousness," (2 Timothy 3:16)

If any church hopes to convince us of another way of understanding the Bible, there better be a dump-truck load of evidence from the Scripture. Thing is, if there was that much evidence in the Scripture, someone would've seen it a long time ago.

The biblical verses the WMSCOG quotes to support their beliefs are scant and inadequate, and they crumble when looked at in context. If the WMSCOG is going to accept these verses as evidence for Mother God, then they also have to accept **Hosea 4:5** where God says:

"I will destroy your mother."

Was God a domestic abuser?

Of course, the WMSCOG would never accept Hosea 4:5 as having anything to do with Mother God. Most likely, they'd say I took the verse out of context.

Exactly.

A STATEMENT OF CONCERN

If I come across as blunt, it's because I believe the Bible is the Word of God so I take it seriously when someone distorts it. That being said, I have the utmost concern for the members of the World Mission Society Church of God. I believe the members of the WMSCOG are hungry to know the true God, but false prophets and teachers have led them astray and their eternal souls are in danger. I pray this book will lead them to the true Gospel of Jesus Christ.

APPENDIX #1

Who is the "Queen of Heaven"?

Though I didn't encounter this on the WMSCOG's website, a friend of mine who had an interaction with a young woman involved in the WMSCOG said to him that the Bible speaks about the "Queen of Heaven." I'm familiar with these verses she referred to, and they're about a pagan goddess named Astarte (or Ishtar).

I've written an article about this before called "Did God Have a Wife?" Read it below.

Did God have a wife? Was she edited out of the Old Testament?

YAHWEH & "HIS ASHERAH"

The idea that the Jewish God was believed to have a wife at some point in history exists because some inscriptions on archeological artifacts from the Iron Age appear to connect Asherah, an ancient pagan fertility goddess, with the God of Israel, Yahweh.

The inscriptions ask for blessings from "Yahweh and his Asherah" (or "asherah," since its unclear if the word is a proper name or not). The artwork may even depict "Yahweh" with Asherah. Of course, the writers of the Bible never speak of the immaterial, self-sufficient, self-existent, one-and-only God of the Jews as having a wife (and making idols and images of their God was strictly forbidden... and how do you make an image of an immaterial being anyway?)

76

But some have even gone so far as to propose that God's wife had been edited out of the Bible.

GOD'S NAME

In Exodus 3, when Moses asks God for his name, God replies, "I AM WHO I AM" and "Thus you shall say to the sons of Israel, 'I AM has sent me to you'" (Exodus 3:14). "I AM" in the original Hebrew is "YHWH" or Yahweh. When you see "LORD" spelled in all capital letters in your Bible, the original Hebrew reads "YHWH," God's name as given to Moses. (God's "name" is really a description of his eternal, self-sufficient, self-existent nature, but that's a discussion for another time.)

THE EVIDENCE (OR LACK OF)

Richard S. Hess, professor of Old Testament and Semitic languages at Denver Seminary, in the article "Did Yahweh Have a Wife? Iron Age Religion in Israel and Its Neighbors" in the book *Come Let Us Reason*, examines the archeological evidence concerning Yahweh, Asherah, and other Iron Age deities. Examining archeology from such a long time ago is difficult because it's like having few puzzle pieces of a large puzzle. For this reason alone, the conclusions the scholars jump to on TV shows like the History Channel's *Bible Secrets Revealed* about Yahweh having a wife are hasty and based on speculation.

Further, no evidence whatsoever — whether early manuscripts or otherwise — supports the idea that the writers of the Bible at one time taught that God had a wife and that this information was later removed. This is purely unfounded speculation and sensationalism.

Likewise, Hess says the evidence never describes Yahweh as having offspring or being connected to fertility religions, and "Asherah's complete absence in all the blessing formulae of letters and all other Judean references to deity" shows she wasn't a prominent figure. In fact, she doesn't even appear to hold any "clear place in the official cult(s)" of the nearby nations. Further, the evidence shows Yahweh with unique "chief god" status in Israel, much different from neighboring pagan lands, and the worship of Yahweh was "somewhat" exclusive in ancient Israel and "virtually exclusive" in Judah.

Hess also concludes from the evidence that Yahwah was not generally identified with physical objects, animals, or other images and idols, and Yahweh's very nature was unique among the Iron Age gods. Thus, the artwork of Yahweh and Asherah — if that's what, in fact, it is — and the inscriptions are oddities, not the norm. Just as it happens today, people try to mix all sorts of false beliefs into the true faith of Christianity. This is one of the reasons it's so important that we have written Scriptures, unlike most of the ancient pagan religions, so our beliefs are secure and cannot be corrupted.

WHAT THE BIBLE TELLS US

Thus, the available evidence supports what the Bible writers tell us: Yahweh was the exclusive God of Israel, but sometimes there was syncretism (the mixing of religions) with neighboring pagan lands. Within the Old Testament, we see constant warnings against Israel mixing with the religions of their pagan neighbors and Israel's failure to listen. We also see references to Asherah-related idols, often in the forms of some sort of trees or "poles."

For instance, Deuteronomy 16:21 commands, "You shall not plant for yourself an Asherah of any kind of tree beside the altar of the Lord your God, which you shall make for yourself." In 2 Kings 21, evil King Manasseh practices idolatry, worshipping other deities other than the one true God, and we're told he "erected altars for Baal and made an Asherah." Then, in 2 Kings 23, King Josiah brings the Hebrews back from idolatry to proper worship of Yahweh by ordering the destruction of pagan idols, including Asherah poles.

THE QUEEN OF HEAVEN

Moreover, the references to "the queen of heaven" in Jeremiah 7:18 and 44:19 may be referring to Asherah, but more likely are referring to a similar fertility goddess (Astarte or Ishtar) of Assyria or Babylon, who was the wife of one of their gods (Baal or Molech). A pagan religion giving a goddess the title "queen of heaven" is nothing unique and doesn't automatically connect that goddess to the God of Israel in anyway, especially since "heaven" is a general term for an astral, non-physical realm. Once again, jumping to the conclusion that Yahweh had a wife from this reference to a pagan "queen of heaven" is a rash conclusion to say the least.

As with many of these unorthodox claims, the idea of "God's wife" is based on little evidence, ignores the Biblical text, and promotes misinformation based on speculation, sensationalism, and canyon-sized jumps of logic.

*Main Source: Richard S. Hess, "Did Yahweh Have a Wife? Iron Age Religion in Israel and Its Neighbors" from the book *Come Let Us Reason*, Digital Edition, v.1, ed. Paul Copan and William Lane Craig, (Nashville, TN: B & H Publishing Group, 2012).

APPENDIX #2

DENOMINATION VS. CULT
What's the Difference?

How do we identify "Christian" cults? What's the difference between a cult and a denomination? What do the biblical writers warn about false teachers?

Warning: False Teachers & Prophets

In the New Testament, Jesus Christ warns of false teachers and prophets who will corrupt his Gospel, his good news of salvation.

For example, in **Matthew 7:15**, Jesus warns:

"Beware of false prophets, who come to you in sheep's clothing but inwardly are ravenous wolves."

Not only Jesus, but the apostle Paul, who wrote much of the New Testament, gives considerable space to warning against false teachers and prophets.

In **2 Timothy 4:3-4**, Paul writes:

"For the time will come when they will not endure sound doctrine; but wanting to have their ears tickled, they will accumulate for themselves teachers in accordance to their own desires, and will turn away their ears from the truth and will turn aside to myths."

81

Furthermore, Peter, Jesus' most prominent disciple of his original twelve, took time to warn against false teachers too.

In his letter **2 Peter 2:1-3**, he warns:

"But false prophets also arose among the people, just as there will be false teachers among you, who will secretly bring in destructive heresies, even denying the Master [Jesus] who bought them, bringing upon themselves swift destruction. And many will follow their sensuality, and because of them the way of truth will be blasphemed. And in their greed they will exploit you with false words."

John, writer of the fourth Gospel, Revelation, and three letters in the New Testament, another one of Jesus' original twelve disciples and arguably as prominent as Peter, also warns about those who corrupt the message of Jesus' good news:

"...do not believe every spirit, but test the spirits to see whether they are from God, for many false prophets have gone out into the world." (1 John 4:1)

And while we're at it, take a moment to read the letter by Jude, Jesus' brother... Do it right now. It's barely one page.

So, here we have throughout the New Testament, Jesus, Paul, Peter, John, and Jude all warning against false teachers and prophets. If Jesus, Paul, Peter, John, and Jude didn't take corruption of God's word lightly, neither should we.

What Do We Mean By "Christian" Cults?

"Cult" isn't necessarily a negative word, such as when used in ancient Rome or in types of Hinduism. It can simply mean a system of religious devotion towards a specific person, god, or object.

But in modern Western society "cult" is a word no one wants to be associated with. Today, in the West, often "cult" means a small group of people on the fringe of society who hold to some strange religious beliefs. But sometimes these small groups of people with odd beliefs grow into large groups of people with odd beliefs.

So, let's be clear about the intended meaning of the use of the word "cult" in this (and the next) appendix article.

"Cult" – more specifically "Christian cult" – will refer to religious groups that have Christian origins or have borrowed from Christian beliefs but have deviated from Christianity to such an extreme that they can no longer be considered Christian.

These religious groups either deny or have changed core doctrines of Christianity so they're not just another denomination. Yes, there are many denominations in Christianity, but the differences between them have to do with different interpretations of minor doctrines and/or differences in their governing leadership. Conversely, cults deny major doctrines – essential doctrines – of the Christian faith.

Why are they "Essential" Doctrines?

By "essential," we mean essential for salvation from sin. By straying from these core doctrines, the cult members don't have salvation from sin as taught by the New Testament Scripture. They have altered, corrupted, or denied the true Gospel of Jesus Christ by altering, corrupting, or denying God's free gift of salvation. Thus, peoples' eternal souls are at stake.

Have no doubt, in using the word "cult" we're stating that these groups are teaching – to use a term that's no longer fashionable – heresy. Though we believe the people in these cults are sincerely seeking relationships with God, they have been led astray by the founders and leaders of these cults, who are – to use more unfashionable language –apostates, i.e. false teachers and prophets.

But the good news is no one is beyond God's grace – not even messed up sinners like me, you, or cult members. That's the good news of Jesus Christ.

But Don't Call Them "Cults"!

I realize what I'm writing in this section is ironic:

Though the word "cult" is used in this article (and will be used in future articles), I don't believe we should use the word "cults" when speaking with members of "Christian" cults (such as blatantly telling someone, "Your church is a cult!"). As stated above, the word has such a negative connotation, the person will take offense and, after that, any chance of an open, loving dialogue will be lost.

Remember, Christians are to speak not just truth but truth with love (Eph. 4:15-16; 1 Cor. 13:1).

How Do We Identify "Christian" Cults?
+, −, X, /

One of my seminary professors, Dr. David Sills, professor of missions and anthropology, gave us a fool-proof way to understand, explain, and remember what makes a group not a denomination, but a "Christian" cult: Use the symbols: **+, — , x, /**

That is:
+ (Addition sign), − (Subtraction sign), x (Multiplication sign), / (Division sign)

This is what each symbol represents:

(+) Adds to the Word of God

(−) Subtracts from the Deity of Jesus Christ

(x) Multiplies the Requirements for Salvation

(/) Divides the Cult Members' Loyalty Between the Cult Leader(s) and Christ

These are pretty straight-forward, but let's break them down:

(+) Adds to the Word of God

Christians believe the Bible, both the Old Testament and New Testament, are God's unique Scripture. There are no other scriptures than these, and there is no need for any more scripture than these. Scripture records God's redemption of humankind from sin, and this was accomplished when God came as Jesus of Nazareth and died on a cross as the perfect, final sacrifice for the sins of the world. Now, according to the commands of Jesus, Christians spread his Gospel and wait for his Second Coming, when he will bring the Final Judgment and restore creation.

Case closed.

Throughout the Bible we see that God confirms his messengers through "signs and wonders" — miracles. The New Testament was completed in the 1st Century by Jesus' apostles. Any addition to God's Word is not God's Word, and any new "scripture" claiming to be from God is not from God. God will not be giving any new scripture because there is no need for it. The church "closed" the canon of Scripture for exactly this reason: so no one could claim to have written, received, or discovered new Scripture. Likewise, to eliminate or change anything from God's Word is corrupting God's Word. Additionally, any "translation" that is not faithful to the original Greek and Hebrew falls under this category.

(−) Subtracts from the Deity of Jesus Christ

Christians believe Jesus of Nazareth, as taught in the New Testament, is God the Son incarnate. Primarily through

Jesus' deeds he displayed his divinity and oneness with God the Father. In every way, Jesus is God. He has been eternally part of the Trinitarian Godhead; he isn't a created being. Only by being both fully God and fully man could Jesus live a perfect, sinless life and accomplish salvation for all of humankind by his death on the cross.

To deny Jesus is anything other than God means Jesus could not accomplish salvation for all of humankind, which means salvation from sins is not possible. Thus, to deny the divinity of Christ Jesus is to be unsaved.

Often "Christian" cults make Jesus (God the Son) less than God the Father. Jesus is seen as a sort of demigod or an exalted angel — a being *created* by God.

As a related matter: Yes, the doctrine of the Trinity – the persons of God the Father, God the Son, and God the Holy Spirit as one God – is hard to wrap our finite, human minds around, but the Bible attests to it. Many "Christian" cults deny the Trinity by either denying the full deity of the Son/Jesus or the Holy Spirit or both.

(x) Multiplies the Requirements for Salvation

The New Testament writers teach that salvation from sins comes only through Jesus' sacrifice on the cross. When someone understands this, they repent of sins, accept this free gift, and follow Jesus Christ – God the Son – as their Lord and Savior.

Thus, no one earns salvation. It's a free gift from God that can only be either accepted or rejected, as with all free gifts. Despite what many think, one doesn't come into God's presence by being a "good person." All have sinned and fall short of the glory of God (Romans 3:23). God's salvation can't be earned, and none of us deserve it. It can only be accepted.

This is the beautiful good news of Christ Jesus – the truly unique message of Christianity that no other faith teaches. To add anything to this simple and beautiful message of salvation is to deny the Gospel of Jesus Christ.

But cults add some sort of "works" to salvation; salvation must be gained, even if the cult holds up some version of Jesus as a savior. The cult members must be deemed worthy of salvation through their works and close adherence to the cult's teachings – and often its solely up to the cult's leader(s) to deem who's worthy of salvation or not.

(/) Divides the Cult Members' Loyalty Between the Cult Leader(s) and Christ

Jesus Christ is the Lord and Savior of all true Christians. God has graciously given us the Bible – the Old and New Testament – as our guide for knowing God's will. The Bible is also our guide for testing the teachings of the teachers of God's Word. If any teacher – whether pastor, priest, or pope – purposely misrepresents God's Word, he is putting himself in the place of God; he is putting his authority above God's.

In cults, the founder(s) and leader(s) are the final authority, not God or Jesus nor their Holy Scripture. They claim to be the only ones who can properly interpret God's Word, or they claim the authority to add to or alter God's Word. To do this is to stand between a person seeking God and God.

88

Like John the Baptist, true teachers of God's Word point their hearers to Jesus Christ. They don't get in the way. They encourage their pupils to read God's Word on their own and strive for understanding. False teachers point not to Christ, but to themselves. And often unquestioning loyalty is demanded.

More Common Characteristics of Cults

These, also, should "raise an eyebrow" if you come across them:

The One True Church

Yes, different denominations have disagreements on minor doctrines, but they don't usually accuse the others of being heretics and devoid of Christ's salvation. Cults often claim they're God's only true church and members of all other Christian churches are destined for damnation.

Often they claim Christianity has been corrupted some time in the far past, but they have the true, restored Christianity as Jesus Christ intended it.

Secret Teachings

Jesus Christ preached in public, performed miracles in public, and both Christian doctrine and Christian churches are open to all. There are no secrets. Cults, on the other hand, often have secret teachings or rituals that only those indoctrinated into the cult know or are allowed to participate in – or even to witness. Often, these are some of their stranger beliefs that they don't want the general public to know about.

Frequently, those new to the cult purposely aren't exposed to these stranger beliefs until they have invested themselves into the cult.

Old Heresies, New Faces

Many of the teachings of these cults are old heresies, meaning they're nothing new. If you look at Christian history, the early church has already faced and addressed many of the same unsound, erroneous interpretations of the Bible these modern cults promote.

"Christian" cults put peoples' salvation through Jesus Christ into serious jeopardy. A cult may have all or any one of the characteristics mentioned above.

APPENDIX #3

Interacting with "Christian" Cult Members: Tips & Strategies Anyone Can Do

How do you respond to friends, family, and neighbors who are involved in a church teaching a corruption of the good news of Christ?

In this article, we'll look at some general strategies for interacting with cult members, whether they're strangers or friends or whether they're standing on your doorstep or sitting across from you in the lounge at work. Afterwards, you will find a checklist to remind you of everything we cover here. You may want to jump ahead and look over the checklist before reading the following.

Interacting with Cult Members

KNOW YOUR FAITH

- **Know your Scripture!**
- **Know why we can trust the Bible!**
- **Know your Christian theology!**
- **Study apologetics!**

The tips above may seem so obvious they're not worth stating, but sadly many Christians can't explain – and certainly can't defend – their faith well. Listening to a sermon once a week isn't going to cut it. Resist all you want, but Christians must be readers – not just of the Bible, but of works that help us understand the Bible.

Furthermore, all Christians should be familiar with Christian theology and apologetics – the defense of the Christian faith – since often cults have their own apologetics that argue that Christianity has been corrupted and their cult holds the one true, correct version of Christianity. Some cults train their members well in their own erroneous theology and apologetics.

Luckily, there are also plenty of websites and blogs with easy, free access, and for those of you who want to read as little as possible, there are some great Christian podcasts out there, such as *Stand to Reason* with Greg Koukl, *the Dividing Line* with James White, *Apologia Radio*, *Backpack Radio*, and *Reasonable Faith* with William Lane Craig.

At the very least, I highly recommend buying a good study Bible (I recommend the ESV Study Bible) and reading up on textual criticism (the study of how the Bible has been handed down to us from the original manuscripts). For this, I recommend *How We Got the Bible* by Neil Lightfoot, a quick, easy but thorough read. I also recommend picking up a copy of *Systematic Theology* by Wayne Grudem and a book on **biblical theology**, the study of the Bible's story as a whole. I have found both *What is Biblical Theology?* by James M. Hamilton Jr. and *According to Plan* by Graeme Goldsworthy extremely helpful.

At first glance, Wayne Grudem's *Systematic Theology* is intimidating because it's thick, but it's extremely readable and thorough. Even if you never tackle reading the whole thing, keep it as a reference tool. Why do we believe Jesus is God? It's in there. How did Jesus' death atone for our sins? It's in there. Wondering about the End Days or the inerrancy of Scripture? It's in there.

CHECK YOUR ATTITUDE

- **Speak to them out of love.**
- **Remember: This is a person pursuing God, & made in God's image.**
- **Be aware of your body language.**
- **Don't call their faith a "cult"!**
- **It's easy to get heated, defensive, & even sarcastic with cult members. Don't.**

First, remember that you, as a follower of the true Christ and led by God's true Scripture, have no reason to feel defensive or threatened. Knowing what you're talking about (as we discussed above) will give you much more confidence, but even if you feel as if you don't have a strong grasp of the Bible or Christian theology, you should still feel secure in your salvation and the truth of Jesus Christ. Feeling confident and secure will keep you calm.

Always remember most of these cult members are honest, everyday people just like you, who are looking for meaning and truth in life and a relationship with God. Sadly, false teachers and prophets have led these people astray. Cult members, like all of us, are made in God's image and have infinite worth to God, so treat them accordingly. Also remember that you received salvation by God's grace alone. You didn't earn it or deserve it. It was only through the Holy Spirit that you were called out of darkness, so stay humble.

Be aware of your body language. Though you may be listening silently, your body language and facial expressions speak volumes, clearly revealing what you're thinking to the cult member. Rolling your eyes, bursts of breath from your nostrils, raised eyebrows, smirks, and furrowed eyebrows aren't going to open anyone up to a loving conversation. If nothing else, remember the golden rule: treat others as you want to be treated. Your job isn't to berate, judge, or demean cult members; your job is to speak truth in love, praying the Holy Spirit will use this to lead them out of darkness and into God's presence.

Finally, if you're having a conversation with a cult member, don't use the word "cult"! Calling them cult members or referring to their church as a cult will accomplish nothing positive. It's an offensive term and, after that, any chance of an open, loving dialogue will be lost. Remember, Christians are to speak not just truth, but truth with love (Eph. 4:15-16; 1 Cor. 13:1).

CLARIFICATION

- **Don't stereotype, generalize, or assume.**
- **Ask them questions: Why do you believe that? Where is that in Scripture?**
- **Ask them to define their terms.**

Just like Christians don't like it when people stereotype them or non-Christians portray their faith inaccurately, other people, of course, don't like it either – including cult members. Remember, the goal is to have an open, loving dialogue, not demean the other person. Even if you know some information about their beliefs (even if you read it in this very book!) do not assume you know anything. Remember, the person in front of you is an individual and an image-bearer of God, just like you.

Before (lovingly) challenging them on anything, first make sure you have a clear understanding of what they believe. Ask a lot of questions, truly listening, and echo back to them their words to check for understanding. Saying "Correct me if I'm misunderstanding you, but you're saying..." is a great way to show you care about what they have to say and to make sure you're not misrepresenting their beliefs.

"Why do you believe that?" is an essential question for you to ask. So, if the cult member says their founder is the Second Coming of Christ, simply ask this question. Their answer will lead to other obvious questions to ask. If the cult member makes any strange claims about what's written in the Bible, simply ask, "Where is that in the Bible? Can you show me?"

If you're astute, you can also ask strategic questions that lead the person to thinking out things they may have never considered before, such as inconsistencies in their doctrine. Greg Koukl has written a great book about how to remain friendly and non-aggressive in a discussion while still challenging the others' beliefs called *Tactics: A Game Plan For Discussing Your Christian Convictions*, which I highly recommend.

Finally, this is very important: Ask them to *define their terms* because what they mean by a certain word or phrase may not be what *you* mean when you use the same words. Just ask, "What exactly do you mean by...?" A cult member might say he believes Jesus is divine. Great. Case closed, right? Wrong. Once you ask, "What exactly do you mean by 'divine'?" you may find out he means Jesus is a demigod, not fully God – and then you have work to do. A cult member might say he believes in "the Trinity" only for you to find out "the Trinity" to him means God the Father, Uncle Pete the Son, and the Holy Spirit Horse of Chief Seattle.

When interacting with cult members, your first goal is listening and collecting information.

USING SCRIPTURE

- **Look at verses they quote in context.**
- **Scripture interprets Scripture: Clear passages clarify ambiguous passages.**
- **Don't fuse over minor doctrine; stick to major doctrines.**
- **Always bring it back to Scripture: especially the Gospel & salvation.**

The first two bullet points above were discussed in Chapter 2.

Don't fuse over minor doctrine; stick to major doctrines.

Cults also have the tendency of making huge deals out of minor doctrines. Yes, Christian denominations disagree on the interpretation or practice of some minor doctrines, but often cults take their interpretation of these doctrines (often unusual takes on these doctrines) and make obedience to them a requirement for salvation.

For example, a cult may state the only true way to be baptized is in natural flowing water with your head bowed. To be baptized in any other way than this, they claim, means one is not saved.

Now, I'm with the Baptists on the doctrine of baptism: the Bible clearly teaches baptism is done once someone accepts Jesus Christ as Lord and Savior; it's an outward, symbolic act to bear witness to others that the one being baptized is declaring Christ as his Lord and Savior; and, finally, "baptism" means "immersion" so those being baptized should be dunked fully in water. Do I believe this is the correct interpretation of the biblical text and we should obey it? Yes! Does this mean those who accept Christ as Lord and Savior but who aren't baptized in this exact way are unsaved? By no means! If someone lives all of her life in a dessert where there is not one pool of water big enough to be fully dunked in, does that mean she remains unsaved? Again, by no means! Salvation comes through God's grace and faith in Jesus Christ alone.

All that being said, don't bother arguing with cult members over minor doctrines. They're often just a distraction from the big issues and the big doctrines – the essential doctrines and beliefs – which salvation *does* depend on (as laid out elsewhere in this book). Focus on the big doctrines, and if you make major progress on those and win a cult member to Christ, then celebrate! There will be plenty of time to discuss minor doctrines later.

Likewise, sometimes cult members make odd claims, like saying Jesus was hung on a stake instead of a cross. Though many of these claims can be disproved, choose your battles wisely and stay focused on the essential issues for salvation.

Always bring it back to Scripture, the Gospel & Salvation.

Always bring it back to the true Gospel of Jesus Christ and the salvation that can be received only through him. Always bring it back to the true word of God. The cult member may be dropping absurd claims on you like a dump truck, but stay calm. You have the truth, so what's there to fear? Even if the cult member is a deft debater, just keep referring him back to Scripture, God's true Word. As long as you're speaking God's truth in love and praying for the intervention of the Holy Spirit, you can't go wrong.

STRATEGIES EVERYONE CAN DO

- **Don't worry about "winning the argument" — just speak truth in love.**
- **"I'll look into that for you…"**
- **10 minutes/10 minutes**
- **Share your testimony & the Gospel.**
- **Pray for them.**
- **Invite them to church.**

Finally, maybe you're nervous about facing-off with a cult member even in a friendly manner; maybe you don't feel confident with your way around the Bible enough to recall all the verses to dispute their claims; or maybe you're simply an introvert who avoids disagreements at all costs. First, let me just say that I can absolutely understand all of these reservations.

Studying the Bible is a lifelong endeavor, so there are always gaps in our knowledge. (But all the more reason to work for a better grasp of biblical, theological, and apologetic knowledge.) Further, I've never been one for confrontations. I grew up doing my best to avoid any conflicts that may arise with others. But these last tips should assist anyone, no matter how introverted and non-confrontational or inexperienced and unschooled.

Let's look at each one-by-one:

Don't worry about "winning the argument" — just speak truth in love

You may not be a trained debater or apologist, but every Christian knows truth, can speak truth, and can speak that truth with love. And remember: speaking truth is important, but actions speak loudly as well. Don't worry about winning an argument. Show that you're concerned for them and their eternal soul. Tell them the truth lovingly and leave it at that.

"I'll look into that for you..."

Perhaps you're fortunate enough to have an open, honest discussion with a cult member, and you're even doing a pretty good job of challenging their beliefs, but then they throw something at you that you don't know what to make of. More than likely, it'll be a Bible verse you've never thought much about before. There's nothing wrong with humbly saying, "That's an interesting point. I can't answer that for you right now, but let me get back to you. I'll look into it." Then, take a look at a good study Bible, ask your pastor about it, and do some other research.

10 minutes/10 minutes

This is a great strategy that shows mutual respect. Simply tell the cult member (who may be standing on your doorstep), "I'll gladly listen to you for ten minutes – allowing you to speak without interruption – if you then do for me the same courtesy and listen to me for ten minutes, allowing me to explain my beliefs uninterrupted."

Share your testimony & the Gospel

Maybe you don't feel deft at spitting out Bible verses verbatim from the top of your head (few do, even experienced pastors), but all Christians can (or at least should) be able to share the reason why they're Christian and explain the Gospel of Jesus Christ.

Pray for them & invite them to church

These may seem obvious, but don't forget to do these two essential things.

Remember, we're called to share the Gospel, but we don't convert people; that's the job of the Holy Spirit. So, do your best to share the truth and love of Jesus Christ and don't forget to pray, pray, pray for the cult members.

CHECKLIST:
Interacting with Cult Members

(1) KNOW YOUR FAITH

- Know your Scripture!
- Know why we can trust the Bible!
- Know your Christian theology!
- Study apologetics!

(2) CHECK YOUR ATTITUDE

- Speak to them out of love.
- Remember: This is a person pursuing God, & made in God's image.
- Be aware of your body language.
- Don't call their faith a "cult"!

(3) CLARIFICATION

- Don't stereotype, generalize, or assume.
- Ask them questions: Why do you believe that? Where is that in Scripture?
- Ask them to define their terms.

(4) USING SCRIPTURE

- Look at verses they quote in context.
- Scripture interprets Scripture: Clear passages clarify ambiguous passages.
- Don't fuse over minor doctrine; stick to major doctrines.
- Always bring it back to Scripture: especially the Gospel & salvation.

(5) STRATEGIES EVERYONE CAN DO

- Don't worry about "winning the argument" — just speak truth in love.
- "I'll look into that for you..."
- 10 minutes/10 minutes
- Share your testimony & the Gospel.
- Pray for them.
- Invite them to church.

RECOMMENDED RESOURCES

Biblical Interpretation:
- *A Basic Guide to Interpreting the Bible* by Robert H. Stein
- *40 Questions about Interpreting the Bible* by Robert L. Plummer.

Cults:
- *The Kingdom of the Cults* by Walter Martin (Ed. Ravi Zacharias)
- *The Four Major Cults* by Anthony A. Hoekema

Biblical Christianity:
- ESV Study Bible
- *Systematic Theology* by Wayne Grudem
- *What is Biblical Theology?* by James M. Hamilton Jr.
- *According to Plan* by Graeme Goldsworthy
- *The Forgotten Trinity* by James R. White
- *Four Views of the Book of Revelation* (multiple authors)

The reliability of the Bible:
- *How We Got the Bible* by Neil Lightfoot

Discussing your Christian faith:
- *What Your Worldview?* By James N. Anderson
- *Tactics* by Greg Koukl

Podcasts:
- *Stand to Reason* with Greg Koukl
- *The Dividing Line* with James White
- *Apologia Radio*
- *Backpack Radio*
- *Reasonable Faith* with William Lane Craig

God From the Machine Blog:

godfromthemachineblog.wordpress.com/

www.facebook.com/godfromthemachineblog

Made in the USA
Charleston, SC
09 October 2014